Lucy's
MISADVENTURES

Lucy's
MISADVENTURES

Stories from a Redbone Coonhound

Anne Teesdale

Sucker Creek Press

A portion of the proceeds from this book will be donated to Friends of the Jordan River Watershed, a nonprofit group whose mission is to "conserve the natural resources and protect the environmental quality of the Jordan River and its watershed." Home to diverse plant and animal communities, the Jordan River Watershed includes some of the last remaining wilderness areas in Northern Michigan.

PUBLISHED BY SUCKER CREEK PRESS

Copyright © 2018 by Anne Teesdale

SUCKER CREEK PRESS
Charlevoix, Mich.

ISBN: 978-1-7324194-0-7

Printed in the United States of America

Cover and text design by tothepointsolutions.com

To Lucy and Trixie, whose adventures and escapades enriched our lives and kept us laughing and crying in frustration.

To John Teesdale, my husband, best friend, and partner in all our many adventures, good and bad.

To all the dogs who shared their lives and love with us, each one unique and special in their own way.

To all dogs who need a home, and the people willing to give stray dogs a chance.

Contents

About the Author

Anne deserves some credit for helping me write my memoirs, so I would like to take this opportunity to say a few words about her.

Anne currently lives in Northern Michigan with her husband, John, where they enjoy sharing their love of the outdoors with their grandchildren. I don't know much about Anne's life before I moved in, but I heard her tell stories about raising her sons in a place called Minnesota, where she helped take care of injured birds and animals at a wildlife and raptor rehabilitation center.

When I knew her, she worked as a veterinary technician at the Jordan Valley Animal Clinic. She would often take me there to get vaccinations, which she claimed were for my own good; or to pull porcupine quills from my face; or to suture me up when I got hurt. I didn't like it there, but Anne said getting regular healthcare was one of the rules of living in the house. And besides, they always gave me yummy cookies to eat.

Anne also had other ridiculous rules about living in the house: I was not allowed on the bed if I had encountered a skunk and I had to suffer through a bath whenever I rolled in some sweet-smelling forest perfume. But again, I put up with the rules because snuggling on the couch with Anne and John made it all worthwhile.

Anne and John enjoy hiking and cross-country skiing, especially when Trixie and I accompanied them. We were able to point out features they would otherwise miss, such as the presence of squirrels, mudholes, and the carcasses of fish and animals.

They are also involved in environmental groups to protect natural areas and habitat for animals. I appreciated their concern, even though they sometimes left us at home to attend meetings.

All in all, life is good.

Love,
Lucy

Introduction

Hi! My name is Lucyfur Devil Dog, but my friends call me Lucy. I'm a Redbone Coonhound. I live with Anne and John and my best friend, Trixie, a black Lab. I moved in when I was about eight months old.

Trixie was about the same age when she came here to live. She was born in New Orleans and thought it was way too hot down there. So, during spring break, a few months before the Big Storm, she jumped into a car owned by John's son, Scott, and hitched a ride north. She thought living in a frat house with seven college guys had some definite advantages—lots of pepperoni-and-sausage pizzas and plenty of beer—but the accommodations were not to her liking. The guys did not have a couch for her to sleep on and everyone was too busy to throw sticks for her for hours on end. So, Trixie chewed the carpet. Scott understood the message and brought her up north to live with his dad and Anne, where life was good.

There are also two annoying birds who live with us. I'm sure they are not supposed to be here, even John agrees with me. I actually managed to catch the noisiest one. He was forever flying low over my head and taking baths in my water bowl! I don't know how anyone can live with his constant chatter. And the more I bark at him, the noisier he gets! One day, I made a spectacular leap into the air and grabbed him. Finally, an end to the incessant chattering. I was sure Anne and John would be thrilled by my achievement; after all, no one else had been able to catch him. Anne, however, was not favorably impressed. She actually made me spit him out! The other bird bites—I have scars on my nose to prove it. But enough about them.

Trixie and I live inside the house with John and Anne. We have our own couch and chairs and bed to sleep on (although sometimes we have to share them with the humans). We have our very own door, so we can go outside whenever we want. I can even stand in the door with my head outside so I can survey the yard without actually going all the way out. This has some obvious advantages, especially when it's raining. Sometimes John gets concerned that I'm letting all the cold air inside. But honestly, he needn't be worried. My ears might get a little chilled, but the rest of me stays plenty warm.

Trixie has three things she likes to do. She likes to chase and wrestle with sticks, play tug-of-war with me, and eat. Once she chewed a hole through a new unopened bag of our food, stuck her nose inside and ate as much as she could reach (she has a very long tongue!). She ate so much she could barely move. When Anne and John came home, Trixie was flopped on the floor, wiggling and wagging her tail in greeting, but she couldn't stand up! Anne said she looked like a bloated wood tick. I thought the whole scene was funny—until they went out and bought some awful diet dog food that both Trixie and I had to eat for a month.

Some of my favorite activities include long runs in the woods, visiting the sushi bar/hair salon on the beach at Lake Michigan (more on that later), playing tug-of-war with Trixie, and long naps on the bed. I also love meeting new people and animals and exploring new places.

Since I am a coonhound, I can travel great distances and always find my way back home. My travels have provided me with some interesting experiences. For instance, one beautiful summer day at the beach I wandered off to do some exploring while no one was watching and found a family having a picnic. They let me stay for awhile and play with their kids. I even got to eat some of their delicious food when no one was looking. They didn't seem too appreciative, though, when I licked their baby. I couldn't help myself; he had barbeque sauce all over his face, and it was delicious.

Another time when I was exploring, a big thunderstorm suddenly came up. The lightning was so bright it hurt my eyes and the booming sky was terrifying! I knew I would have gotten soaked if I had run all the way home, so I ran up to the nearest house and barked until they let me inside. They were very nice and insisted that I stay and have some cookies with them. They even called Anne and John to come get me so I wouldn't have to get wet in the storm.

Then there was the incident at the llama farm. I prefer not to discuss that one, though. John and Anne don't know the details and I'd just as soon keep it that way. They weren't too happy with me when they found out I'd wandered over there. But honestly, they didn't need to be concerned. Nothing *really bad* happened. And I got away relatively unscathed. And a very nice lady gave me a ride home in her car!

All in all, life is good. Every day is a new adventure, which is why I've written this book. I hope you enjoy reading about some of my more memorable experiences.

Love,
Lucy

The Joys of Giving

Anne and John left the house early one morning to help pick up trash in the Jordan River. I decided to follow their example and do a little volunteer work of my own. So, I jumped over the fence in the backyard and ran down the street to the Rainbow Shop (a used-clothing store).

Although I could not get inside the store, I was able to stand on the sidewalk and greet people as they walked by. You have no idea how happy people are when they see a cute dog run up to them, jump on them, and give them wet, sloppy kisses! Some people screamed in delight when they saw me approaching! And the people who worked there were so impressed with my job performance they phoned Anne and John several times to tell them where I was.

Unfortunately, John and Anne were in a canoe on the river and didn't have their phones with them; so, they didn't listen to the voicemails until later. They were so glad to see me when they finally arrived home. I could tell because John kept yelling about having to skip lunch and drive seventy miles an hour down dirt roads just to get to me sooner.

Anne was concerned because I had cut my foot jumping over the fence and it was bleeding. I told her it was nothing to worry about, but she insisted on taking me to the veterinary clinic where she works to suture it. She gave me something to help me sleep; when I woke up, I discovered she had wrapped my foot in a pink bandage! I hate pink, so I chewed off the bandage as soon as she wasn't looking.

All in all, a great day for everyone.

Love,
Lucy

It's a Cat! Get the Gun!

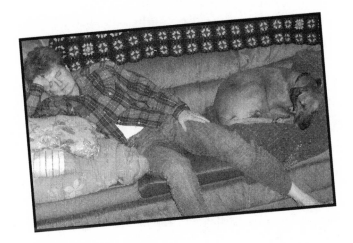

John and Anne didn't realize there was a flaw in their fence design, which allowed me to patrol the neighborhood at night (when they thought I was sleeping). I knew the fence was important to them, so I decided to take on the job of pointing out its more obvious engineering defects. (More about the fence in another story.).

One night, when I was almost home from night patrol, I realized there was a cat in the area. This was a high-alert situation, so naturally I barked loudly to alert the neighborhood of the danger. I chased the cat into our neighbor's shed, and continued to bark, THERE IS A CAT IN THE SHED! FOR GOD'S SAKE, DOESN'T ANYONE REALIZE THE GRAVITY OF THE SITUATION?!

No response! I barked louder.

Anne finally heard my alarm and came outside to help—but WHERE WAS THE GUN?!!! She was totally unprepared for the situation. And confused. Apparently, she thought I was trapped inside the shed and couldn't get out. She pried open the door and proceeded to climb over piles of discarded furniture, appliances, lawn equipment, and toys to get to me. At this point I realized she was not going to be of any help. She was just getting in the way and her yelling made it hard for me to concentrate on the cat, which was, after all, the reason we were inside the shed. I barked at Anne, "Don't worry, I'll handle this. I've got the situation under control."

But the more I barked, the more determined Anne was to reach me.

She finally managed to grab my collar and drag me out of the shed. As she led me back into the house, she was muttering about needing to get some sleep because it was three in the morning. I could tell she was concerned about my rest, but she didn't need to worry. After all, I could sleep all day.

Needless to say, this big misunderstanding allowed the cat to escape. Well, there will always be another opportunity.

Love,
Lucy

Eyeglasses—A Delicious Treat

I got the "Devil" in my name shortly after the incident with John's eyeglasses. Honestly, I didn't know it was his favorite pair. I found them on the floor (after I accidentally nudged them off the coffee table). Since they were now on the rug with my toys, I figured it would be okay if I tried them out. They looked like a delicious change of pace from rawhide chew bones.

John did not agree. A loud crunch woke him up, and he jumped off the couch and proceeded to chase me from room to room while yelling at me to drop the glasses. It was easy to stay out of his reach, though, because he kept running into tables and chairs! It was as if ... he couldn't see very well!!??

As I momentarily stopped to contemplate that thought, he made a lucky grab and got me by the throat. I couldn't breathe with his hands wringing my neck, so I was forced to spit out the glasses. I thought John would be happy to get them back, after all, I found them to be rather tasty. But he was actually quite upset. He yelled that I had ruined them and he couldn't drive the car without them! Suddenly, it occurred to me that if he couldn't drive then we couldn't get to the park for our walks!

Chewing up eyeglasses was a mistake. I will try hard not to do it again.

Love,

Lucy

Agility Classes

When I was younger, Anne took me to agility classes. She seemed happy when I jumped over the obstacles and climbed things. At class, all I wanted to do was bark at the other dogs, but she would smile and hug me whenever I climbed over the A-frame and jumped over the gates.

Eventually, I realized these were good skills for any dog and I naturally decided the purpose of the fence in the backyard was to allow me more quality practice time to perfect my skills.

I really impressed John and Anne with how quickly I learned to climb over the fence. In fact, they spent several entire weekends making the fence higher just to provide me with a greater challenge! When I learned how to dig under the fence, they provided me with new obstacles, such as wire and large boulders to make the digging more interesting and to increase my problem-solving abilities. I really impressed them when I figured out how to pull the wires of the fence apart with my teeth and make a hole right through the fence.

Of course, once I was on the other side, it only made sense that I should do a little exploring. I had many great adventures in the swamp behind our house. Once I found a strange creature that didn't run very fast. Naturally, I ran up close for a better look. He actually slapped me with his tail! It felt like being stuck with a hundred porcupine quills! Oh wait, it was a porky-pine—I've seen them before. I wonder if they all have those annoying prickly quills. The last four porcupines I encountered certainly did.

It was also fun to run down to the big road and meet new people. I love meeting new people. Eventually someone always stopped and gave me a ride in their car and brought me home. Anne and John didn't like it when I hitchhiked, but I told them not to worry, all people were friendly. I have tons of experience with this.

The last time I jumped the fence, they were quite angry. Then it occurred to me, maybe the purpose of the fence was to keep me in?!

For the past few months, I've been allowing them to think the fence is working; and they seem more relaxed and happier. And we go for walks in the woods every day, so I'm content.

Love,

Lucy

Night Patrol

Anne and John finally fell asleep. I slipped out the dog door and scaled the fence, anxious to get started on my neighborhood night patrol. Almost immediately, I encountered a strange-looking black-and-white kitty. Naturally, I began to bark. It's my job to alert the neighborhood to the presence of ... well ... anything that moves.

Now, I know a lot about cats. I've had tons of experience. I know they all love to be chased by dogs. But, this one didn't run. It was rooting around in the dirt, eating seeds and grubs. Being naturally curious, I barked louder and moved in for a closer look. We were almost nose to nose before he turned his back to me. I thought, Oh, boy. Now, the chase was on! I barked louder in anticipation.

But instead of running, it lifted its tail and sprayed me in the face with some smelly, yellow, gooey liquid! It was awful! Some of it got in my eyes and it really burned. I could hardly see! I had to forget about the kitty for the time being and run home.

I hurried inside—I have my own private door, remember. I jumped on the couch and rubbed my face on the cushions, frantically trying to get the stuff out of my eyes. It still stung, so I tried the arm of the chair next.

Amazingly, Anne knew what had happened! How could she know? She was asleep in the bedroom! She grabbed a bottle and flushed my eyes out with water and wiped the goo off my face. My eyes stopped burning and I felt so much better!

By then, I was ready for a nap and headed for the bedroom. But Anne grabbed me by the collar and insisted I have a bath first. I tried to tell her I felt much better, thanks to her quick action, and was really much too exhausted for a bath, but she insisted. She said I didn't smell too good. I told her not to worry, I didn't think I smelled that bad, and besides, it would wear off before long.

In spite of my strong protests, she unceremoniously threw me in the bathtub and shampooed me with some awful-smelling stuff she uses on her hair. I struggled and shook, trying to get the icky soap off my fur. I finally managed to jump out of the tub and escape. I proceeded to run frantic circles through the house. After all, how could I relax when I smelled like herbs and flowers?!

But wait, I knew what to do next. I ran out my door and into the yard and found a nice patch of dirt and rolled around in it several times. I felt better almost immediately!

Then I snuck back inside, jumped up on the bed, turned a few circles to get the blankets scrunched up just the way I like them, and finally, I got to lay down for a well-deserved nap.

I heard Anne and John muttering about wet, stinky dogs as they came back to bed, so I decided to scoot down under the covers so wouldn't know I was there. They seemed annoyed.

Love,

Lucy

P.S. I wonder if all black-and-white-striped cats spray goo. The last three I encountered certainly did! I will have to investigate this interesting phenomenon in more depth.

Who is the Smartest?

Although Trixie is a year older than me, I am definitely the smartest. For instance, I like to snuggle on the blanket right between John and Anne at night when we're watching TV. The more they squish me, the more I like it.

One night, I got up for just a minute to get a drink of water—and when I returned, Trixie was in my spot! I stood there for a moment, looking in disbelief! How could this be??? I whined and barked, trying to explain to her in a rational manner that she had taken my spot and she should move *immediately*. Trixie did not listen to reason; in fact, she totally ignored me.

Didn't anyone see the injustice of the situation!? I whined louder (whining helps me organize my thoughts). Then, a plan came to me. Of course! Why hadn't I thought of this sooner?

I grabbed a tug-of-war rope from the toybox and proceeded to fling it around, back and forth, in front of Trixie. No response. I moved in closer and dropped the rope right in front of her. She still didn't move, but I could tell her resistance was weakening. I picked up the rope again, growled for extra effect, and shook it as hard as I could.

Finally, she couldn't stand it any longer. Trixie jumped up and grabbed the rope—the game was on! We both growled and pulled and growled and pulled, and eventually I was able to maneuver her out to the middle of the floor, away from John and Anne and the blanket. Finally, I was in position! A quick glance over my shoulder and I knew my moment had come. I dropped the rope jumped on the blanket in my proper spot, and snuggled between Anne and John with a contented groan. Trixie just stood there looking confused, still holding the rope in her mouth. That trick worked so well, I have used it several more times, all with the same satisfying results.

There is one area, however, where Trixie is more skilled: the art of counter surfing. Whenever I sample something delicious from the counter, Anne and John always know I did it; something about broken dishes on the floor. But Trixie, well, she is masterful. She can eat a whole stick of butter off the plate without moving the plate even an inch! Anne and John never suspect a thing. They just go out and buy more butter! I even saw Trixie eat half of a pumpkin pie without pulling the pie tin on the floor. Now, that is true talent! I wish she would teach me how she does it, but Trixie is usually not in a generous mood when food is at hand. But that's okay. I love her anyway.

Love,
Lucy

Barking—One of My Many Talents

I must confess, I LOVE to bark. And, I'm quite good at it. I often bark simply for the joy of hearing my own voice. Anne and John sometimes yell at me for barking so much. They seem to think I will damage my vocal chords from overuse. I try to tell them not to worry. After all, I can bark at squirrels all day long when they are not at home, and no bad effects have ever occurred. In fact, all those hours of practice have actually improved my skills!

John once read an article about coonhounds that claimed many people find coonhounds' voices to be melodic. Anne and John both laughed when he read that part, probably from happiness at knowing there are other dogs out there who sing as beautifully as I do.

Aside from being a form of artistic expression, barking also serves a utilitarian purpose. I've learned from experience that barking gets the attention of those around me, sometimes to my advantage. For instance, Trixie and

I are supposed to get a rawhide chew every night at nine o'clock. Since Anne occasionally gets involved in watching TV and forgets, I must bark to remind her. It works every time. Barking also works to get Trixie's attention when I want her to drop a toy or play tug-of-war with me.

But I didn't realize just how powerful a tool barking could be until one day when we were on our walk in the woods, Trixie and I came across a porcupine. I've seen them before—fascinating creatures! I wanted to get a closer sniff, but it ran up a tree. The tree was thin and not tall, but the porcupine was still just out of my reach. So, I did what I do best. I barked. I barked and barked. And I barked louder. John came running toward me, and he was yelling something, but I couldn't make out the words over the racket of my own voice.

Oh well, I can always talk to him later. I continued to bark. And then, an amazing thing happened. Barking really works! Once again, incredibly, barking got me what I wanted! THE TREE BROKE AND THE PORCUPINE FELL TO THE GROUND!!!!!!!! I ran in for a closer look and was nose to nose with it when ...

John grabbed me by the collar and yanked me away as he shook his head and said, "Don't you remember what happened the last time you got too close to a porcupine?"

"Oh yeah," I said. "Now that you mention it, I do remember Maybe it's a good thing you stopped me."

But still, I couldn't help thinking, Behold, the power of my voice! I was quite impressed with my abilities.

Love,

Lucy

Anne and John Get Lost

Anne, John, Trixie, and I were on our daily walk in the woods when I came upon a most intriguing creature. It was big, with antlers, and I really wanted to get a closer look, but it saw me approach and ran. Oh boy, I thought, a chase! I love a good challenge! I was so excited, I barked for everyone to follow me. If we all worked together, I was sure we could catch it.

I took off in hot pursuit, over a hill. I didn't have time to explain the situation to Anne, John, and Trixie. I had to trust that they understood my instructions and would follow me. I chased the deer through the woods, dashing over logs and up and down hills. We jumped over a creek, ran through the swamp, and through more woods. I had to admit, that buck was really fast.

In spite of my best efforts, he was getting farther and farther ahead, and I was getting winded. I paused momentarily to catch my breath and to confer with my team about our next move. But, where were they? I looked around. ***Where was my backup crew? They were nowhere in sight!*** I thought my instructions to them had been quite clear. Oh well, maybe they couldn't keep up and decided to head the deer off from the other direction.

I trotted along, following the trail a while longer. Another hour passed, and still no sign of Anne, John, or Trixie. Hmm, what could have happened to them? I knew it would be impossible to catch the deer by myself, so I had to give up the chase. I was really quite tired, and it was getting near dinnertime, so I headed back to the car. Along the way, I chased two rabbits, a chipmunk, and countless squirrels. I investigated a fox den; stopped by the creek for a long drink of water; and took a nice, relaxing mud bath in the swamp to cool off.

Several hours later, I finally made it back to the parking area and the car ... but ... still no sign of Anne, John, and Trixie! I knew I should go back in the woods to look for them, since they were obviously lost, but I was so exhausted, I couldn't take another step.

Just then, a very nice man stopped his car and asked if I was lost. I knew exactly where I was, but before I could answer, he opened his car door and said he'd take me home. Actually, that wasn't such a bad idea. After all, it was past dinnertime, and I was soooo awfully tired. I showed him my address—I always carry my phone number and address with me on my collar. It has come in handy many times. He drove me home and opened the gate for me. I ran up onto the deck and inside the house. He was even nice enough to leave his business card inside my dog door, in case I should ever need his chauffer services again!

I looked around the house. Still no sign of Anne, John, or Trixie. They must be lost. I hoped they would find their way home soon because it was past dinnertime and I was famished. I decided to take a nap while I waited. I jumped on the couch, scrunched the blankets up just so, and got all snuggled down and comfortable. I must have dozed because I didn't hear John walk in the door until he yelled, "WHERE HAVE YOU BEEN??? WE'VE BEEN LOOKING ALL OVER FOR YOU!!!" He carried on about how I was lost, and Anne and Trixie were still out there, looking for me.

I wanted to interrupt, to point out the obvious: I was not the one who was lost. I was home, while Anne and Trixie *were still wandering around in the woods in the dark!* Maybe he should be out looking for them, instead of yelling at me. But I decided it was best to keep my opinions to myself. John obviously wasn't in the mood to listen to reason.

He finally left in a huff, to look for Trixie and Anne. I offered to help, but John said no, I had already done enough. I took that as a good sign, maybe he was calming down a little and was finally able to appreciate all my effort and hard work.

Soon enough, we were all together again, enjoying a well-deserved meal, and a good night's sleep. Tomorrow we will be ready for a new adventure.

Love,

Circling and Barking

One evening while exploring in the woods, Trixie and I found an interesting creature sitting on the ground at the base of a tree. Naturally, we had to investigate. Trixie let me approach first, probably in deference to my superior hunting skills and problem-solving abilities. My job was to assess the situation, formulate a plan, bark my instructions to Trixie as to what our next move should be, and …"OH, NO! OUCH!" I yelped. Darn, it was a porcupine! My nose was full of quills, and they really hurt. I jumped back and pawed at my face, trying to get them out, but it just made my nose hurt worse.

Oh, well. No time to dwell on that now. The porcupine was on the move, and Trixie and I had work to do. We circled and barked, and circled and barked, as the critter slowly ambled across the trail. We continued to circle and bark, as it meandered past five or six trees and into a thicket of raspberry bushes. It was exhausting work, but we never gave up.

Oh, oh. Anne was running toward us. What was she thinking?!! Didn't she realize she was putting herself in danger? I barked to warn her to stay back and leave this job to the professionals. Trixie and I knew what we were doing. Anne would simply get in the way. But she wouldn't listen. And then—oh, no! My worst fears were realized. Anne tripped and was falling right over the porcupine! It tried to scurry out of the way as she crashed, headfirst, into the brambles. Anne slowly stood up and shook the dirt and leaves out of her hair. Then she let out an ear-splitting scream. "OMG, I'VE GOTTEN QUILLED!!! They really, really hurt!" she yelled, as she pulled two quills out of her arm.

Now that Anne had experienced how painful quills could be, I was sure she'd be sympathetic to my plight. But instead, she blamed the whole situation on me!!! How could that be? She should be angry with the porcupine. After all, he was the one who walked by several perfectly good trees and didn't bother to climb any of them. This unfortunate incident could have been avoided had he simply gone up a tree. Because of the porcupine's irresponsible behavior, Trixie and I had no choice but to circle and bark and circle and bark.

Anne was not in the mood to appreciate our diligence and dedication to duty. Oh, well. No time to dwell on that now. I needed to focus on the job at hand. Trixie and I continued in our mission ...

In spite of my best evasive maneuvers, Anne finally managed to grab my collar and drag me away. I barked to Trixie to maintain vigilance. I would find a way to break free and return to help her. But Trixie came running as soon as Anne called her. She said she'd much rather chase sticks than porcupines.

As we walked into the house, John exclaimed, "*OH, NO! QUILLS AGAIN?* Doesn't this make time number eight?"

No. Technically, it had only been six times. The two times I rolled on dead porcupines should not count. But John was sometimes prone to exaggerate.

The next thing I knew, John had me in a half-nelson headlock while Anne pulled out the quills. They hurt more coming out than they did going in. I struggled to get away, but John was stronger and I couldn't break free. Trixie, untouched by quills, watched from a safe distance.

Finally, the terrible ordeal was over. I got lots of hugs and kisses, and I had to admit my mouth and nose felt much better. After dinner, Trixie and I curled up on the couch for a well-deserved nap. As I drifted off to sleep, I wondered if that porcupine would still be there tomorrow. Maybe I'd let Trixie go first next time ...

Love,
Lucy

Trixie and the Cows

It was a beautiful, sunny, August afternoon, perfect for a walk down the dirt road by our house. Trixie and I split up, each of us feeling the need to pursue our own interests.

I decided to investigate an interesting muddy depression amidst the trees. Rabbits often frequented the area, and I was primed and ready for a good chase should the opportunity arise. If not, then a cool, refreshing roll through the mudhole would be a welcome relief from the hot sun.

Anne and John, who were with us, usually stayed on the road; fortunately, they didn't know what I was about to do because I was quite sure they would not have approved.

Trixie, on the other hand, almost exclusively thinks about food, and the aromas that day were rich and intoxicating. She caught the scent of one particularly sweet smell—cow pies! She crawled under the electric fence and followed her nose into the field of tall grass. It did not take long for her to find what she was looking for. There were several cow pies; some still steaming hot, to choose from. Trixie carefully inspected each one and made her choice, completely oblivious to her surroundings as she anticipated the feast in front of her.

She took one delicious bite—but before she could even swallow it, Trixie realized she was not alone. She raised her head and saw the large eyes of fifteen cows surrounding her.

Yikes! she thought. *They are BIG!* She temporarily lost interest in the buffet, and suddenly realized that John and Anne were frantically yelling at her to come back. But since she was surrounded by large bovines, escape to the safety of the road looked futile.

As the audience of cows watched, Trixie raised every hair on her back. This display was meant to make her look big and scary and fierce; designed to strike terror into the hearts of her adversaries. *Surely the cows will run away now*, she thought.

For a moment, it was so quiet, you could hear crickets chirping. The cows stood their ground. Trixie's legs began to shake. One particularly large cow stared at Trixie and let out a loud snort; then she reached down, grabbed a mouthful of grass, and began chomping. The other cows agreed. It was time to eat.

Apparently totally unimpressed with Trixie's display

of fierceness, the cows lost interest in her and resumed gossiping among themselves and chewing their lunch.

Trixie slowly backed up, glanced over her shoulder for a break in the crowd, and made a beeline out of the field, leaving the cows to chuckle as they watched her unceremoniously skedaddle back to the road.

Love,

Lucy

Night Patrol—Once Again

My night job of barking at would-be intruders can be exhausting. I'm not complaining though. I'm good at what I do and I enjoy the opportunity to test my skills while providing a useful neighborhood service. The last few nights had been busy, so I was actually planning on taking this particular night off. All of us were looking forward to a good night's sleep. However, it was not to be ... an intruder was in the yard!

Without a second thought to my own safety, I ran outside to confront the danger. Naturally, I began to bark. The alien glared at me with yellow eyes and fierce-looking teeth. It was a raccoon. I knew this would be a tough fight. I barked louder and chased him up a fencepost. The situation was now critical. I lunged at the raccoon but missed by inches. He hissed and growled and swatted at me, reluctant to leave the supply of sunflower seeds he had found in the birdfeeder.

I barked furiously, bobbing and weaving, ducking under his teeth and claws, waiting for my chance to get him. Several neighborhood dogs heard my alarm and began to bark in solidarity, urging me on. Just then, Anne came outside and announced that she wanted to talk to me. This was NOT a good time for a conversation, I barked back. We could talk later.

She must not have understood me, because she started to run toward me with a flashlight in her hand. She was heading straight into grave danger! Couldn't she see the severity of the situation? Somebody was going to get hurt if I didn't act quickly, so I made a valiant lunge at the raccoon. I would have had him, except Anne ducked under the raccoon and grabbed me around the chest and dragged me away.

I struggled and barked and twisted and turned, trying desperately to get loose from Anne's grip. We were almost to the door, when Anne dropped me and screamed that she was scratched and bleeding! I knew that raccoon would hurt someone. I raced back across the yard to prevent more bloodshed.

Then, John came running outside. All he had on were his boxer shorts! What was he thinking? It was cold out and he doesn't have much fur to keep him warm. Again, just as I lunged at the bloodthirsty critter, John grabbed me around the neck, preventing me from breathing. I had no choice but to go with him because I was starting to turn blue. But, I had managed to chase the raccoon away, so all was not lost.

Whew, what a night! We were all pretty tired after that excitement. I headed for the bedroom to get some sleep, but Anne and John slammed the door shut before I could get in.

Oh well, I should probably stay out on the couch and maintain vigilance—in case the raccoon returned for more sunflower seeds.

Love,

Lucy

Barf

The morning started out normally. Trixie and I ran with Anne to the end of the driveway to get the newspaper and to check out all the fresh rabbit tracks in the yard. We ate a nice breakfast, played a quick game of tug-of-war with our rope toy, and then it was back to bed under the covers to cuddle with John.

I was just getting warm and comfortable when ... uh-oh, there was an awful rumbling in my stomach. I quickly jumped out of bed, dragging the blankets with me. John grumbled, "Where did all the cold air come from?" But I didn't have time to listen. I ran out the dog door onto the deck and proceeded to yak up my breakfast.

Anne said that's what happens when I eat "disgusting

things"—her words, not mine. Well, actually, last night I did find a delicious raccoon poopsicle. I couldn't roll in it because it was frozen. This time of year, you have to find them hot out of the oven, so to speak, if you want to use them as perfume. Poopsicles were delicious, and I enjoyed it thoroughly. How could something so scrumptious make me feel so awful? Oh, well, no time to think about that now.

Two steaming, juicy piles of regurgitated breakfast were in front of me and they were all mine. Trixie was still asleep on the bed. Darn, Anne just looked out the window and noticed what had happened. "Oh, you poor puppy. You don't feel good," she said when she walked onto the deck. Actually, I felt much better. But before I could say a word, she ran back in the house yelling, "Wait right here! I'll get some Pepto-Bismol to make your tummy feel better."

I had to work fast. Two steaming-hot piles ... I quickly gobbled them down. Yum, yum! I felt much better! Regurgitated food tastes just as good, if not better, then it does the first time. I was just savoring the last bite when Anne returned with that yucky pink stuff.

"Where is all the barf?" she asked. *"OMG, you ate it all?!!! That's gross!!!"* she exclaimed. I thought she'd be happy that I had cleaned it up so she wouldn't have to do it. Plus, she would have just thrown it in the garbage— what a waste! But, instead of appreciating my efforts, she grabbed me by the collar, pried open my mouth, and proceeded to pour in the yucky pink goo. It tasted terrible, so I shook my head and flung out as much as I could.

Anne no longer seemed sympathetic to my plight. As she ran back in the house to clean the Pepto-Bismol off her clothes and hair (apparently my fault), she yelled that I was making her late for work. I decided to go back to bed. As I settled in, I hoped my stomach would stay calm. I didn't think I had enough energy to run back outside should the need arise.

Love,

Lucy

Sushi Bar

One of my favorite activities, especially in the summer, was to visit the sushi bar/hair salon at Lake Michigan. I discovered it one day while we were on one of our walks through the woods. Trixie and I were busy chasing squirrels. One particularly noisy squirrel flicked his tail at me, challenging me to a chase. We zigzagged over logs and around a brush pile toward a big tree. I almost had him when ... the wind changed direction. I stopped dead in my tracks as I got a whiff of the most intoxicating aroma floating up from the beach! I forgot all about the squirrel as I was totally captivated and had to follow where my nose was leading me.

I bounded over the crest of a sand dune toward the

water and there it was—a big, beautiful salmon that had been marinating in the sun—and I found it first! Oh, the joy! The anticipation! I ran up to it and eagerly tasted the delicious sushi. Mmmm, mmmm, mmmm. Just the way I like it. A delectable treat. I gobbled down as much as I could, until I absolutely couldn't eat another bite.

I wanted to savor the aroma for as long as possible, so I decided to apply a little of the carcass to my fur. After all, besides smelling wonderful, salmon contains many essential fatty acids necessary for a shiny coat. But, I had to work fast. Anne and John would be coming over the hill at any minute, and I was pretty sure they wouldn't approve. I got my shoulder in position just so, then rolled several times over the fragrant fishy pile. Back and forth I rolled, allowing the gooey goodness to soak deep into my skin. A little more goo applied just right to my neck and collar—I was in heaven.

Uh-oh. Anne and John were running in my direction, waving their arms in the air and yelling, "No! No! Not again!" I decided to skedaddle away so they couldn't drag me away from this wonderful place. I ran down the beach with the wind in my face and the sun on my back. I felt on top of the world. I knew I looked and smelled fantastic. The other dogs I encountered agreed, as they crowded around me, trying to sniff my neck and admire my shiny coat.

Eventually, John and Anne reached me. Anne was not so favorably impressed and insisted on giving me a bath as soon as we got home. I tried to explain to her that it was okay if we didn't agree on fragrance choices. After all, I never complain about how her hair smells after she uses her herbal shampoo. But, she wouldn't listen to reason and proceeded to drag me to the tub as soon as we were home. I twisted and turned and tried to get away, but she finally managed to wash away all of my hard work.

Later, I realized that maybe getting a bath wasn't such a bad idea. After all, who wants to wear the same fragrance two days in a row? A bath would give me the opportunity to explore new fragrances tomorrow. The woods provides a wonderful smorgasbord of tastes and smells, and I've found many to be suitable appetizers and hair conditioners. Eventually, I hope to find one that Anne and I can both agree on.

Love,

Lucy

P.S. For any of you dogs who wish to try rolling at home, I say, be creative! Try everything! Find something that works with your individual taste and hair type. I would, however, caution against rolling on dead porcupines. The aroma can be enticing, and the carcass may appear to be a great back-scratcher, but trust me, the quills tend to stick in the skin. Both times I rolled on dead ones, I experienced the same disappointing side effects.

Roll away, have fun, every day is a new adventure!

Camping Trip

O h, boy! Oh, boy! Yippee!! This is going to be a great day! Anne and John have all the camping equipment out and they already packed our dog food! Hooray! We are going camping! We can't wait!!!

The thirty-mile drive to the top of Dead Man's Hill in the Jordan River Valley was taking forever. Trixie and I anxiously paced and whined in the backseat. John had constructed a board to keep Trixie and me from jumping into the front seat. It never made sense to me because we always alerted him to interesting things to look at, such as squirrels, dogs, and clumps of trees. It was certainly more efficient for us to provide that service from the front seat. But John complained about nose prints on the windshield making it hard for him to see. So, Trixie and I have no alternative but to constantly whine, "Are we there yet?"

We were almost at our destination when John made an unscheduled stop ... at a convenience store! What was going on? Trixie and I were not consulted on this.

To make matters worse, Anne and John got out of the car and closed the doors, leaving us inside. We barked, trying to draw their attention to the travesty of the situation. They ignored us and went inside the store. We continued to bark. But then it occurred to me that they had left all the food inside the car! I decided to investigate this interesting situation. I tried to enlist Trixie's help getting the sandwich meat out of the bag, but she wasn't interested, so I proceeded on my own.

Trixie was intent on finding a better vantage point from which to bark, so she jumped over John's well-constructed dog barrier into the front seat. She landed on the box of raspberries that Anne had carelessly left on the console between the seats. The box tipped over, spilling red, ripe raspberries onto the seats. Normally Trixie would have stopped at this point and eaten the evidence—she will eat anything. I, on the other hand, have more discriminating tastes. I honestly don't understand how humans can eat some of the things they put in their mouths. Seriously, blueberries and raspberries, tomatoes, oranges, spinach? Yuck! Although I do occasionally enjoy a sweet carrot or a banana. But generally, for a special treat, I'll stick to the tried-and-true roadkill café. Nothing like partially pureed squirrel or rabbit that has marinated in the sun for a few days. But, I digress.

Trixie jumped from seat to seat, barking and stomping

the raspberries deeper into the cloth cushions. Anne finally returned to the car, opened the door, and gasped. "OMG, look at all this blood! What happened?! Who got hurt?" she screamed. She frantically tried to grab Trixie to see where the blood was coming from. "Oh, wait." She answered her own question. "These are my raspberries! All ground into the seats! Yuck, what a mess!" Trixie noted the changed tone in Anne's voice and prudently jumped over the dog barrier into the safety of the backseat.

Anne and John insisted on buying several more rolls of paper towels before we were finally on the road again. I thought about suggesting they also buy more sandwich meat, but they didn't seem to be in the mood for constructive suggestions, so I stayed quiet.

We finally reached our destination and enjoyed a weekend of hiking, swimming in the river, eating camp food and rolling in lush patches of poison ivy.

Love,

Lucy

How to Live a Good Life

This last story is about love, which is everlasting. I lived a wonderful life full of adventure and love. My body may be gone now, but my spirit roams free.

Anne and John cried, but eventually they were able to open their eyes and realize I was still with them. I still go on walks in the woods with them, my spirit floating freely. And I have shared with Anne some of the secrets of life, as I saw it.

Every dog, person, and living being has a song to sing. Listen to the music and embrace the uniqueness of their stories, even if you don't understand them. Love and appreciate—but don't try to change their songs. All dogs, like people, have their own thoughts and feelings, and we all have something to say. I have no regrets. I lived my life to the fullest. I loved the people and dogs in my life, and they loved me. My life was good.

Live life for the moment. Every situation can be an adventure. Find and savor the adventure in every situation. Embrace the unexpected. Often the most exciting experiences are unplanned. Living in the moment is a good way to live life.

Don't be afraid to try new things or to make mistakes. Yes, I've heard the adage "Learn from your mistakes and don't make the same mistake twice." I truly believe that adage is overrated; I do not recommend it. We shouldn't be so afraid of failing that we miss out on the opportunities and adventures in front of us. Approach each adventure as a new experience.

For a good life, love those around you and tell them often that they are loved. Cuddling under the blankets is the best. Give lots of kisses. And let those around you feel like they are in charge once in a while.

Appreciate each new day. Love the sun, the rain, wallow in the mud, play with your friends, and go swimming whenever the opportunity arises.

Love Always,
Lucy